a coping mechanism
naomi polonia
illustrations by malcolm cantor

sophia & malcolm,
thank you for your endless support.
i never would have done this without you.

table of contents

1

preface

i was thirteen years old when i wrote my first poem. it was in a composition notebook i used for social studies vocabulary the year prior. that became my *official* poetry book and i would write in it whenever i felt exceptionally inspired.

it was usually when i was sad.

what i wrote at the start of my adolescence wasn't great. it probably wasn't even fine. i haven't opened that notebook in years out of fear of how i'll react to the ~cringe~. but i guess it wasn't supposed to be great, or good, or fine, even. it was a start and that's what matters most. at least i think so.

i was fifteen years old when writing became less of a coping mechanism and more of a thing that brought me joy. purpose. i still only wrote when i felt like i needed to; it did not lose its value as an emotional tool. the things i wrote then are gone now, locked under an email account from a school i no longer attend, a notes app from a device i no longer have.

it no longer brings me pain to know that the words that were once a part of me are gone forever.

i am twenty years old now and i am still writing. i hope to keep finding joy in the way words intermingle with one another. i intend to keep finding safety in this art.

you are about to be immersed in words i kept to myself for years of my life. i hope they are as meaningful to you as they are to me.

thank you for picking this book up. thank you for skimming through it once or over and over again.

and please. don't forget to breathe.

A BLOODSTAINED WHITE DRESS

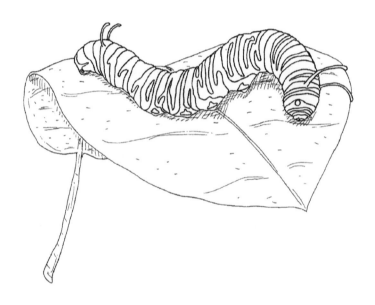

hallowed be thy name—just saying it makes
me wanna choke

being with you felt like saying a prayer—
sacred/intimate/familiar

so sit down for a while. join me in adoration, for once.
light the candle in the shadow of He Who is Most High.
light a candle under—to me—is you. it's heresy, babe, but
when i have heaven on earth maybe i deserve to go to hell.

neither of us have read the epistle to the corinthians

but here we are again, trapped in between the
nothingness and the somethingness, under a stained
comforter
my feet are cold and i press them against your thighs and
you don't complain
this is love, i think
it's our own, though
it's not very patient or very kind and is
self-seeking
in the best way possible (
you only say you love me when you are in my mouth)

forgive me, father, for i have sinned / my last confession was five years ago

here's what no one tells you:
your heart won't beat as fast after the first time
your hands will do more than his
your mother cares more about it than she'll say

here's what no one tells you:
it's grueling and nightmarish
being soaked to the bone in sin

padre pio

a stigmata on my chest plate
off center—a little to the left
the blood doesn't pour, but
it leaks

slowly, but, thankfully, painlessly.

i need to change the bandages twice a day
sometimes i'll forget; only the chosen can see the blood
soak into my shirt. i know because they stare.
i wish i could tell them:

i see yours, too.

xxxxx, king of the unreliability of both love and war

it was a battle, now lost

on display
wearing my crown of thorns

you warned me, i know
you were right, i know
i'm sorry, i know

blood trickles into my eyes now
and i almost laugh—my world, finally rose-tinted

now, better than never

there are times i think i've made my peace with god
and then i think about you.

PICKING OFF NAIL POLISH

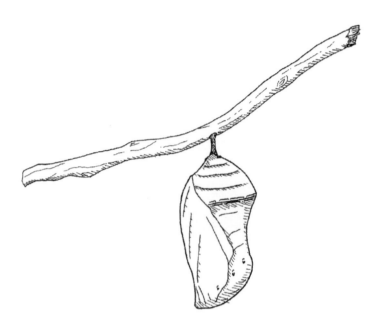

chronicle of a death foretold

you know how a flower attracts bees?
i was helpless to the clear blue of your irises
the ring of gold that haloed your pupils

how a pitcher plant attracts flies?

unearth it all and watch it rot

a tombstone
etched in memoriam for
wasted innocence

a summer of being seventeen. a lifetime of paranoia.
uneasiness. i just wanted to sit, wanted to talk but my
underwear always ended up on the other side of the room
and—

no. no. no!

a syllable each and less than a second to say
but. meaningless? not to me,
god, please, not me

a tombstone
etched in memoriam:
here lies the cadaver of who was once me, adored and
never forgotten
nineteen ninety-nine to two thousand seventeen

rotting from my core
never to look a man in the eyes ever again

i'd rather you hold me under

here's the setting: we're on a dock at the edge of the world

i can't recall what we're wearing but i'm cold and there
are goosebumps on your arm and despite the cracking in
my joints, i can feel my heart
defrost—the freezing water dripping down my lungs and
pooling on my stomach

i'm crying now and you're looking away now and i swear
i'm trying to be quiet but it's hard, okay, it's hard to feel
like your hands are tied behind your back and there's a
brick tied to your ankle and someone's telling you to jump
even though you'd do anything to stay above water.
anything not to drown, but you've got no goddamn choice
when you both went out to buy rope and found a
cinderblock on the side of the road and now you're here

at the edge of the world and i'm still crying god i won't
stop fucking crying because you won't push me off you
won't even

give me that

to the girl who lost her ability to be tender

tell her
it's okay—
her teeth are shards of glass and she is merciless with
them
skin is skin: the inside of her own cheeks, his lips, tongue,
throat, fingers
a broken beer bottle will puncture whatever it touches
and doesn't care if its consequences are stained with
blood

thinking of repercussions is so passé

the consequence?
>   an empty and hollow thing,
>   the size of a fist, in my chest.

WHAT'S LEFT BUT ASH AND SMOKE?

sylvia

i'm a recluse—

sitting in a ribcage
like a canary in a coal mine

a diving board, 6 miles up

eros holds my head beneath water
one two three four fivesixseveneight —
sputtering/coughing/breathing
>   what is love?
>   where is the fire? where is the passion? am i not
>   the sun to his icarus? does my love not burn
>   bright?
again. nine ten eleven twelve
>   i swear not to be spiteful, just dangerous
thirteen fourteen fifteen sixteen
he says,
>   "it is not the blaze of the sun that drowns him,
>   it is the waves."

eight days and twelve hours

it's day three of waking up to you in my dreams
it wasn't a nightmare this time
i'm so glad it wasn't a nightmare this time
i didn't like seeing you ripped from my life—
sharp jagged edges and all
i didn't like seeing you with her—
my heart in my throat, blood bubbling and gushing
up, up, up

i can still taste it

no, this time
this time i had you
and this time you had me, too

merriam-webster

the tips of your fingers are fluent in a language all their
own
touching different areas yield different definitions
different results
you're delicate, tracing from 'hold me closer' to 'maybe
you should use chapstick more often' to 'the shampoo you
use smells nice'
one palm rests against 'i missed you' and the other rests
against 'fuck me' and i realize, to us
they are the same thing

what does all this love amount to?

a dictionary definition, torn out
every word between me and you, erased
replaced with the shadows of our fingertips
on each other's lips, chests
pressed into each other's palms

in the spring, petals fall like tears
there is no shame in loosening in the wind

WHAT I HAVEN'T FIGURED OUT YET

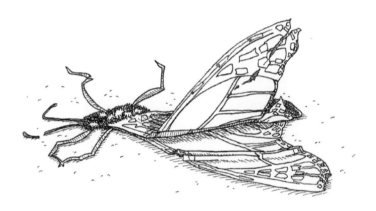

untitled.1

in fair verona where we—
fuck—no that's not right
let me start again
in front of a dimly lit 7-eleven in suburbia, anywhere usa
this isn't a love story, we aren't star crossed, no one dies

well, not really.

this is nail biting and chewing on your bottom lip until it
bleeds
this is the hole in your sock this is a bra that's one size too
small
this is the longing this is the fear and this is when it's too
late and so was yesterday and so was the day before that

a rose by any other name? still has thorns to prick your
fingertips.

untitled.2

to learn that tenderness is a wound
pulsing, dripping
with a mixture of blood and fear
scabbing around the edges

is to become woman

untitled.3

vessel
>/ˈvesəl/ - noun

something that carries something else. it gets heavy. it gets heavy. it gets heavy.

e.g.
<u>hands</u>
>i place strawberries and cool whip on top of a

carton of eggs and orange juice. i try not to crush the loaf of bread under my arm as i feel the strap of a tote bag dig into my shoulder. you told me once that your mother would surprise you with strawberry shortcake in those little cake cups, years ago. i couldn't help but get them.

<u>heart</u>
>i can't keep it full for very long, but it weighs the

same either way. i think it sprung a leak the year i turned thirteen. does anyone know a plumber i could call?

<u>head</u>
>do you ever feel the weight of the world on your

shoulders? it is. now, it is. the bone behind your eyes was soft once, and what lies protected behind it was empty once, too. i don't know if that brings me peace or sorrow.

vessel. can you use it in a sentence?

untitled.4

forgive me—
yes, there is blood running down my chin. no, my teeth
will not retreat back into my mouth

untitled.5

before you, there was a sense of cold feet and looming
dread
a pebble stuck in my shoe
strands of hair tangled in a comb

now
mirrors, reflecting
soft light comes from a window facing north
a pen and lined paper
and finally, our shadows on the wall

"do you think we'll ever feel like this again?"

Printed in Great Britain
by Amazon

72190969R00031